BRITAIN'S HERITAGE

Fire Stations

Billy Reading

AMBERLEY

Acknowledgements

This book is dedicated to the courageous fire fighters of the UK, who remain ready at all times to risk their lives for our safety.

In addition, the author would like to thank the following people: Richard Hurley, Liz Reading, Kathryn Ferry, Nick Wright, Tom Reading, Bob Bonner, Michael Bowman, Steve and Viki Mayes, James Thomson, Fiona Taylor, Maude Audrey, Alisa Moss, Vanessa Fletcher, Hannah Parham and Jane and Beth Scaysbrook.

First published 2017

Amberley Publishing
The Hill, Stroud
Gloucestershire, GL5 4EP

www.amberley-books.com

Copyright © Billy Reading, 2017

The right of Billy Reading to be identified as the Author of this work has been asserted in accordance with the Copyrights, Designs and Patents Act 1988.

ISBN 978 1 4456 6582 5 (paperback)
ISBN 978 1 4456 6583 2 (ebook)

British Library Cataloguing in Publication Data.
A catalogue record for this book is available from the British Library.

Printed in the UK.

Contents

1
Introduction

The fire station is a readily identifiable and well-respected building type around the world. Recognising the simple form of a fire station from its component parts is easy, and with this recognition comes the knowledge that, inside this building, there is a brigade of fire fighters waiting for the call, ready to perform acts of bravery and heroism. This awareness is inherent when we recognise the building type, the history of which, in Britain, can be traced back around 350 years to a time before brigades were provided as emergency services by local authorities.

The need for a dedicated building to house a fire brigade has its roots in the insurance companies of the seventeenth century, as insurance fire brigades came about in direct response to the Great Fire of London in 1666. Before this time the nearest thing to a fire station would be some parish fire buckets and ladders, probably stored in the church porch – a casual approach to storing equipment, and one that was heavily reliant on members of the public to operate it. This had been much the same throughout the ancient world. From the seventeenth century onwards, the 'fire engine house' as a building type began as a simple storage shed or repurposed agricultural building.

With the advancement of technology, firefighting became more formalised, and so the need arose to accommodate bigger and more specialist equipment. Fire brigades became increasingly professional, and the architecture of fire stations had to adapt to reflect this, with both the layout and the architectural expression of the buildings becoming more complex throughout the nineteenth century. As this happens, the term 'fire brigade station' appears, later more commonly abbreviated to 'fire station'.

The golden age of fire station design was the late Victorian era, and we have a wonderful and eclectic legacy of buildings from that period across the country; buildings that tell, in brick and stone, the story of civic pride and technological advances in the firefighting industry.

The twentieth century saw radical changes to the threats fire brigades dealt with and to the equipment available. The buildings again had to respond to this, with increased refinement of plan form to accommodate modern appliances and equipment, combined with increased simplification and standardisation in the architectural form and palate of materials.

While the role of fire fighters and the architecture of fire stations have both changed significantly over 350 years, the basic layout and core functions of a modern fire station would still be recognisable to a Victorian fire fighter. The fire station is an instantly recognisable, specialist building type which plays an important role in the functioning of our towns and cities. Whether we are aware of it or not, our local fire brigade are, right now, in readiness to come to our aid, should we need them. For this reason the fire station remains a key civic building, epitomising bravery and safety in our collective consciousness, both intangibly through the actions of fire fighters and through our shared collective memory, and more tangibly through the physical fabric of the buildings.

2

Early Firefighting Arrangements

The earliest firefighting relied on communities working together with the equipment they had to hand: leather buckets and other vessels, sent to and fro from the nearest available water source by human chain; dampened blankets; rush mats and shovels full of earth to extinguish the flames. Fire breaks would be created to arrest the spread of fire, while burning buildings and those adjacent would be pulled down with hooks, ropes, axes and other commonly found tools – occasionally with explosives.

The vernacular building materials of Britain are timber, wattle and daub plaster and rush, reed or straw thatch. These are all highly flammable materials, through which fires could quickly spread.

The Roman Empire had a documented system of '*Vigiles*' or watchmen, an early system of formalised firefighting. They were organised into teams called cohorts, each with responsibility for a particular area. Each cohort contained a range of different skills, so in the event of fire different people would organise the water supply, the human chains, and the hooks and poles (known as harpagones). Each team also had a doctor. The first written reference to firefighting in the UK comes from a document called the *Notitia Dignitatum*, which mentions a cohort of *Vigiles* in Concangium (Chester-le-Street) in the late fourth century. *Vigiles* used hand pumps or 'squirts', known as '*siphos*'. These were manually operated pumps arranged with pistons and cylinders. Similarly to other early equipment, the siphos was not exclusively used for firefighting but was also used to move water for a variety of reasons. Like buckets and ropes, they would have been part of everyday life in Roman Britain and would have been

The Roman force pump, excavated at Silchester Hill in Berkshire.

quickly deployed should a fire arise. In the fifth century the Roman Empire withdrew from Britain, and so the systems of organised administration, including firefighting, disappeared.

For the next 1,000 years tightly packed towns of timber-framed buildings continued to develop inside defensive walls. Aside from arson as a tool of warfare, accidental fires were generally perceived to be an act of God, divine retribution for immorality and a natural consequence of human sin. Most parishes had some fire equipment in place, largely the same tools available to the Romans. Specifically designed firefighting buckets had a narrower top and a wider base to avoid spillage. These were kept at the church or in the market place. Ladders and hooked poles often leant up against the church tower; the fire station as a distinct type of building still did not exist.

In the sixteenth century, cistern-style fire engines began to provide a more continuous and reliable stream of water for firefighting. The cistern was mounted on a sledge or wheels, with a long-handled pump operated by two people, and a copper nozzle that could be directed towards the fire. These still had to be refilled in situ with buckets, which required plenty of volunteers. The lost Roman technology, the *siphos*, was rediscovered in Europe in the sixteenth century, appearing in Britain after the 1520s and having become commonly known as 'squirts'. This more specialist equipment had to be stored in a building larger than the church porch, and the requirement for a dedicated building arose. These early buildings would be simple structures – a cart shed or a bay within existing stables, most likely an existing building re-purposed as a fire equipment store.

Oil painting, c. 1797, showing the Great Fire of London on its first night. The foreground features Londoners escaping by boat, whilst in the background Old Saint Paul's Cathedral rises above the flames. The cathedral was ultimately destroyed by the fire.

The English Civil War (1642–49) sufficiently increased the fear that fires may again be started as acts of war to the extent that many towns issued fire protection ordinances, or local laws. Evidence suggests many towns reviewed their fire provision during this period – for example, at Plymouth the fire hooks were overhauled, and in 1643 in Coventry ten brass squirts and fifty buckets were ordered. Despite fires being relatively common, a fire of unsurpassed scale and ferocity in September 1666 made it desperately apparent that the ad hoc system of firefighting could not continue, and that changes must be made to the way in which fires were tackled and buildings constructed. The Great Fire of London spurred a significant change to firefighting nationally. The fire began on 2 September 1666 in the bakery of Thomas Farriner in Pudding Lane, a short narrow street leading uphill from the Thames. There had been serious drought that year, and rain had not fallen for months. Strong winds served to fan the flames enabling the fire to spread quickly. Despite there being no organised fire brigade or emergency services, strategies were in place for tackling outbreaks of fire. By this period, London did have some early prototype fire engines and a number of squirts. The first alarm would be raised by shouting, to achieve the safe evacuation of occupants of adjoining houses, then the bells of the parish church would be rung in reverse peals, an alarm that citizens would recognise. The parish constables would block off either end of the street, to arrest the opportunities for looting, which in the ensuing mayhem was a common occurrence. The assembled crowd would then form human chains, passing empty buckets one way and full buckets the other. On the fateful night, however, these strategies did not fall into place and the fire quickly spread to adjacent streets. Attaining an unstoppable momentum, the conflagration burnt out of control for four days, causing widespread panic and ultimately destroying around 13,200 houses in 400 streets and courts, eighty-seven parish churches and many significant public buildings and institutions – including forty-four of the city's livery halls and the iconic, ancient Saint Paul's Cathedral. Somewhere between 70,000 and 80,000 people were made homeless. The costs were estimated at the time to reach upwards of £10,000,000; around £1.1 billion in today's money.

Did you know?

Before the seventeenth century the only form of compensation for those who had lost goods or property to fire was a charitable fund. A plea known as a 'brief' would be read out in church by the priest, and the church wardens would take a collection.

Once the Great Fire was quelled, thoughts turned to rebuilding London. This seemed the opportunity of a lifetime, to rebuild the cramped, illogically planned mediaeval city in a formal and orderly manner so that it would be more resistant to destruction by fire. However the pressing need to get the city back to trading to generate much-needed taxes, combined with a lack of government funds to compulsorily purchase privately owned land, meant that ultimately property owners had to rebuild their houses on their original plots.

The Great Fire spurred improvements in processes and technologies, including an overhaul of the construction industry with the introduction of the London Building Act in 1667. This required buildings to be of brick and stone with slate roofs and with proper brick dividing

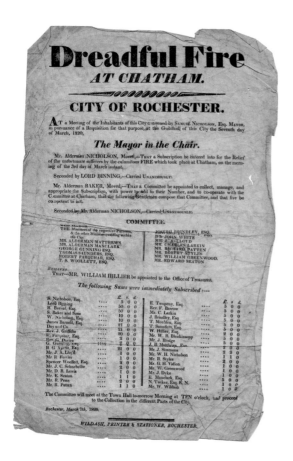

A plea for donations for the relief of the poor, recently disadvantaged by the dreadful fire at Chatham, 1820. The names of the subscribers are included. This much earlier system of charitable donation continued well into the nineteenth century.

walls between each house to prevent the spread of fire; it also specified that the streets should be wide enough to act as a fire break. The Act applied initially only to the walled city of London, although further building Acts of 1707 and 1709 extended the regulations to the City of Westminster, introducing further regulation in regard to brick parapets, the banning of timber cornices, and the stipulation that timber windows and doors should be recessed from the wall line. A further Act in 1774 extended these construction standards to the entirety of the built-up area of London. These London Building Acts became prototypes for other British towns, with legislation commonly introduced following major fires. The stipulation of these Acts gives us the pattern of building that still defines British towns and cities today.

In the wake of the Great Fire, many interested parties advised the King on the formation of a proper fire brigade. At this time parliament was struggling to extract itself from a European war and was resultantly slow to act. The private sector jumped in to fill the gap, led by the notorious profiteer, Nicholas Barbon. As the city was gradually rebuilt so new development spread westward, and Barbon set himself up as London's pre-eminent property developer, laying out new streets and squares along the Strand and in Soho. It was at this time that Barbon struck upon the idea of selling these new houses complete with fire insurance. In order to do this, while maximising personal profit, he set up a fire insurance company called the Fire Office, creating the country's first fire insurance brigade in 1667.

3
Insurance Fire Brigades

Nicholas Barbon's insurance company, the Fire Office, began in 1667 and operated without rival until 1681, when the Corporation of London began to offer fire insurance from offices at the Royal Exchange. This venture was not a success, as evidenced by its abandonment in November 1682. In 1683 a new insurer began a business named the 'Friendly Society for Securing Homes from Loss by Fire'. Barbon's firm clearly felt this company to be a threat, launching acerbic newspaper attacks that pointed out, among other things, that the Friendly Society did not even have its own fire brigade. In 1696 a third insurer began trading, grandly named 'The Contributors for Insuring Houses, Chambers or Rooms from Loss by Fire by Amicable Contributionship', an unwieldy title necessitating the more popular nickname 'The Hand in Hand Fire Office' after its friendly-looking logo. It had officially adopted this popular name by 1706. Likewise the Fire Office changed its name to reflect its logo and became the Phoenix Fire Office in 1705, Barbon having left the organisation sometime before his death in 1698. And although it had the first private fire brigade, the others soon followed. All three of these early brigades issued fire marks to advertise their business on the buildings they insured. A common misconception about these insurance brigades is that they would only fight fires at the buildings they insured, and that they would stand and watch if uninsured

An original fire mark from the Hand in Hand insurance company. The shaking hands, crown and policy number would originally have been painted in bright colours to make it stand out.

The Sun Fire Insurance company fire mark policy 525070, dating from 1769. Traces of red and gold enamel paint can still be seen highlighting the logo.

An illustration showing the operation of a cistern-style fire engine, with volunteers working the handles and refilling the cistern with buckets, and firemen mounting the ladders to direct the hose and rescue trapped residents.

buildings were aflame. This persistent myth was never true. The brigades would turn out to fight any fire that came to their attention, and eventually established a reciprocal arrangement of covering one another's costs if the building was insured by a different company.

The firemen would be retainers, and would come from their homes or workplaces at the call to fire. The first London insurance brigades preferred to employ Thames watermen – that is, men employed in transporting goods and people across the river.

A major player in the fledgling fire insurance industry was the Sun Fire Office, created in London in 1710. Early in its existence this company began to spread beyond the confines of the city, intending ultimately to cover the entire country by creating a network of agents. This model took off during the eighteenth century, and was widely copied by other insurance companies. The first fire insurance outside of London was offered by the Bristol Crown Fire Office, formed in 1718. In 1720 Scotland's first fire insurers, the Edinburgh Friendly Society, initially covered the city and surrounding areas but expanded in 1767 to cover the whole of Scotland. The first Irish insurance company started in Dublin in 1771.

Advancement of firefighting equipment began to change the industry. The Dutch invention of flexible leather hoses in 1673 was a revolution. Early hoses were fabricated from leather folded into tubes stitched as a shoemaker would stitch boots, with brass fittings every 15 feet to allow sections to be joined together and a gooseneck nozzle to direct the jet of water. These leather hoses required significant maintenance; it was necessary to wash and dry them after each use, and to rub in preservatives periodically. The fire engine was also overhauled in the 1680s and '90s, with technological innovation following at an increasing pace into the eighteenth century, by which time several rival fire engine manufacturers had appeared. Expanding under the agent system, fire insurance companies would contribute towards or purchase more specialist equipment and distribute it to areas where they had concentrations of policy holders.

In the latter part of the eighteenth century fire insurance businesses began in many British cities and towns, including Bath, Birmingham, Newcastle, Shrewsbury and York.

A statue of two firemen wearing uniforms, helmets and boots leaning on a manual pump with axes and buckets. Although this statue has moved to its current location in Leamington Spa, Warwickshire, it is believed to be a late eighteenth-century trademark of the Birmingham Fire Office.

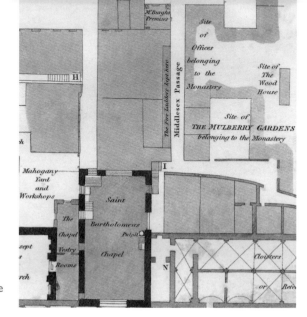

A map extract showing the parish of St Bartholomew the Great, London, in 1821. Note the phrase 'fire ladders kept here' against one side of Middlesex Passage. This is an example of the parish storing their fire equipment in a convenient location.

Most of these companies had their own brigades, with equipped and uniformed retained firemen. As equipment became heavier, horses were increasingly used to pull the appliances. Horses could be fairly easily hired from commercial stables or coaching inns, and the insurance brigades tended to do just this, meaning that hired horses would be fetched separately by an ostler before the brigade could turn out. In Shrewsbury, Shropshire, the Salop Fire Office stored its engine at commercial livery stables on Swan Hill. This was a convenient arrangement, as the insurance offices connected to the stables by an alleyway that came, over time, to be known as Fire Office Passage.

While insurance companies could reasonably well maintain retained brigades in larger conurbations, the costs and the greater distances between insured buildings in smaller towns and rural areas rendered provision more challenging. As insurance companies increased their policies in an area, they would donate

Above left: Birmingham Fire Insurance Company logo, 1805. The most prominent feature is the purpose-built office building of the insurance company, a fine example of classical architecture. The building in Union Street, Birmingham, has subsequently been demolished.

Below: An octagonal building in Barrow upon Soar, Leicestershire, first erected 1827. This structure has been put to a wide variety of uses throughout its life, including hearse house, parish prison and sometime fire engine house. Known as the round house, it is presently used as an exhibition space.

equipment, which would commonly be stored in a civic building near the parish church, or in an adapted agricultural building.

The traditional structure built of cob on the village green in Guilsborough, Northamptonshire, served as the store for fire equipment. Here, the location of the parish church at the far end of the village meant that it did not provide a convenient place, so the more central green became the designated fire equipment store. Later accounts also describe a fire engine being stored in stables adjacent to the village pub, and the structure on the green being used for other community uses, demonstrating that the architecture of the fire engine house was generally undistinguished, traditional and above all, practical.

The owners of large country estates, which were often considerably valuable assets far from large towns, found securing favourable premiums difficult. Their response was to provide their own fire engine to keep in the stables, together with uniforms for the butler and groom, and set up their own private brigades. These 'country house' brigades would even attend fires within the vicinity of the estate, in a purely philanthropic manner. Increasingly many small towns responded in a similar way to devastating local fires

A traditional agricultural building of cob walls on a brick plinth, with thatched and slated roofs, which was once used to store the parish fire equipment. On the village green of Guilsborough, Northamptonshire.

Four gentlemen of the Coventry Volunteer Fire Brigade, 1862, proudly wearing their uniforms of coarse woollen tunics and insignia, as well as black 'glazed' hats – a form of homemade firemen's helmet. The cistern fire engine behind has buckets hanging from the pump handle, and a lamp at the front. This volunteer brigade existed until 1930.

Oilette postcard showing the headquarters of the County Fire Office in Regents Street, London, designed by John Nash. The company, established in 1807, first rented this building in 1819 and it remained their headquarters until 1970.

by creating a volunteer brigade, established by voluntary subscription. These became known as gentlemen's brigades.

The main buildings associated with these insurance companies would be their offices; initially, firms would be more likely to lease an existing building rather than to build their own. Equipment would be stored on the ground floor, or to the rear in sheds and store rooms. They focused resources on the provision of equipment rather than on establishing an identity through commissioning architecture. As companies began to cover larger areas, so the requirement to store equipment in a variety of locations increased. This began with fire engines being stored in rented commercial premises adapted for the purpose, or else in existing civic buildings – watch houses or sheds, as close to commercial stables as possible. Where no suitable premises was available, purpose-built structures to store the fire engine and associated equipment, called 'fire engine houses', began to appear. These buildings are firmly in the vernacular architectural language of industrial or agricultural buildings, designed to serve a practical purpose.

Did you know?

The last private brigade of an insurance company is thought to have been that of the Norwich Union, which turned out for the final time in Worcester in February 1925, bringing 249 years of insurance brigade firefighting to a close.

The first building that could be described as a recognisable fire station was built in London in 1794 at Old Cockspur Street, Charing Cross, for the Phoenix Assurance Company, established in 1782. It was designed by Thomas Leverton (1743–1824), who also built the headquarters of the Phoenix in Lombard Street. An architect's name being associated with this structure marks it apart from the cart sheds of earlier periods. Leverton used the principles of classical architecture to imbue a sense of solidity, implying reliability, strength and tradition. Giant rusticated columns of the Doric order support a decorated entablature bearing the words 'First Station', carved monumentally into the stone. The area was one of aristocratic and royal residences. The statement building was in response to a concentration

Design for the first station of the Phoenix Fire Insurance Co., 1794, Old Cockspur Street, London. The building differed slightly when constructed, but the basic form remained, with the identifiable large arched opening, and the inscription 'Fire Station' (instead of 'First Station') at the top.

of policy holders in the area but was also an attempt to encourage more business and to impress the idea that here was a firm you could trust. This building signalled a new approach to fire stations: firstly, in that the name subtly changed; secondly, in that the building had grown significantly, reflecting the changing functions within; and thirdly, in that it used architectural style to reflect its importance. These changes are important as, at the beginning of the industrial revolution, Britain was covered by a random and unsatisfactory range of localised firefighting. Like so much of Britain's social and commercial life, the status of fire brigades in the UK was set to transform.

4
Municipalisation

At the beginning of the nineteenth century, fuelled by rapid industrialisation, towns and cities grew at an unprecedented rate. The emergence of industrial technologies, and the shift of employment into towns and cities from the countryside, resulted in hastily built and densely crowded residential areas collocated with industrial sites in an unregulated urban environment. The hearth was still central to the home in this period – every household relied on open fires for cooking and heat, and on candlelight. Serious fires were common, and the insurance fire brigade system was struggling to cope.

Suggestions of municipal fire brigades were increasingly discussed at this time, and various attempts to combine insurance company resources were trialled but ultimately failed. The urbanisation of Britain was throwing up new and surprising challenges and many similar questions: who should be responsible for the increasing municipal responsibilities – for paving and sweeping streets, for instance, or for refuse collection? For hospitals, police and fire brigades? Should these services be public and, if so, how should the costs be

borne? These issues were resolved in a piecemeal and parochial way across Britain, with firefighting often falling to the back of the queue as the insurance brigades were offering a solution that had worked reasonably well.

Some debate exists over the formation of the first municipal fire brigade. Edinburgh City Council appointed twelve retained fire masters, each with six assistants at public expense in 1703, although they received no training and the costs were still recouped from building owners in the insurance brigade model. The MPs for Beverley in the East Riding of Yorkshire agreed in 1726 to employ twelve men

The inscription 'Fire Engine House' is barely legible over this narrow arch at the bottom of the poor house in Calne, Wiltshire. The building dates from the mid-eighteenth century, and the parish fire pump was stored here from 1822 to 1888. This would be the hand-pumped cistern-style of fire engine.

to work the existing parish engine. The town corporation formed a committee to manage this arrangement, with representatives from the insurance companies as well as churchwardens – a Georgian example of a sort of public-private partnership. The Beverley system seems to have enjoyed success, as a similar model was adopted in Tetbury, Gloucestershire, in 1745 and by Grantham, Lincolnshire, in 1764. The Belfast Police Act of 1800 behoved the city corporation to inaugurate and maintain a fire service. The immediate purchase of an engine made in London indicates that this took place, although until 1861 this service was part of the police force, with policemen trained to attend and extinguish fires. The unified police-fire brigade was a model later more widely adopted in the UK.

The catalyst for change came in 1824 when Edinburgh suffered an unprecedented number of large fires. The civic authorities were forced to take action and, in merging the insurance companies and setting up the Edinburgh Fire Engine Establishment, which they placed under the jurisdiction of the police commissioners, so began Britain's first proper independent municipal fire brigade. The insurance companies still provided a significant amount of funding, nevertheless; eighty retained firemen were recruited, and the full-time position of Master of Fire Engines was offered to a twenty-four-year-old surveyor, James Braidwood.

Recruits came from the navy, a tradition that continued for many years in brigades around the world. A number

James Braidwood, 1800–61, Master of the Fire Engines of the first municipal fire brigade in Edinburgh, and later superintendent of the London Fire Engine Establishment until his death at the great fire of Tooley Street. He is widely credited as the father of modern fire fighting.

Did you know?

James Braidwood established the UK's first fire brigade in Edinburgh, and is often referred to as the father of modern firefighting. He introduced a rigorous training programme for his firemen, including gymnastic exercises and mandatory drills at 4 a.m. every Wednesday.

of slang naval terms crept into the early fire brigades and remain in use to this day, such as 'crew', 'drill', 'watch' and 'mess'. Perhaps the most enigmatic is the call and response phrase 'Ready?', 'Aye, ready!', which not only became the motto of the Edinburgh brigade, but of a number of Scottish and English brigades as well as others around the world.

Many industrial towns and cities were keen to follow Edinburgh's example. Rochdale set up a municipal fire brigade in 1826, as did Manchester in 1828, Brighton in 1831, Liverpool in 1834 and Norwich in 1835. Still the equipment tended to be stored at the town hall or police station, occasionally in a simple fire engine house.

The rolling out of municipal brigades, and therefore the development of the fire station as a building type, across Britain was slow. The 1830 Lighting and Watch Act paved the way, allowing parishes to use their 'utmost endeavours to prevent any mischief from fire', but this Act imposes no actual responsibility and interpretation of the language of the Act varied.

Insurance brigades, volunteer brigades and country house brigades continued to coexist. Increasingly industrialists saw the benefit of funding their own brigades at mills or foundries. This was especially prevalent in the Midlands, although the Hodges brigade based at a gin distillery in Lambeth, London, is a celebrated example.

Kingston upon Hull in Yorkshire, fire station dating from 1932 using banded stone and brickwork, and with the call and response 'Ready Aye Ready' carved into the stonework over the appliance bays. The balcony and flagpole confer civic authority, and the traditional window forms and tall, hipped roof give a comfortable, traditional feel.

Above: This building served as the Cowbridge Rural District Council Fire Brigade station in South Wales until 1960. It comprises the side elevation of the Cowbridge Town Hall of 1830. With four appliance bays at one time, the building also has a bell tower at roof level.

Below: Marlow, Buckinghamshire, in 1896. The former town hall of 1807 has been mostly taken over by the neighbouring Crown Hotel, but part of the building was given to the town as a fire brigade station. The local horse-drawn fire engine is seen here being filled from a standpipe in the street.

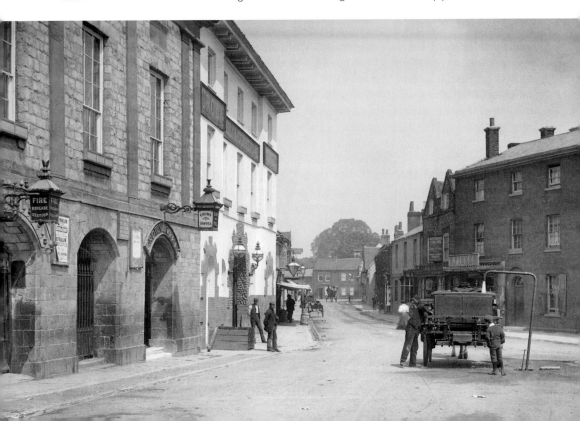

The firemen of the Northenden volunteer fire brigade, Greater Manchester, in the 1870s or 1880s, mounted on a horse-drawn manual pump, wearing uniforms and brass helmets.

In 1830 a proposal came about for the largest insurance firms to combine and provide London with a single firefighting force. In 1832, representatives from ten insurance companies met to discuss the formation of a Fire Engine Establishment for London, in the style of that established in Edinburgh.

By August an agreement was made. The new organisation would consist of eighty professional firemen based at nineteen fire stations, with engines and equipment transferred from the insurance brigades. The funding for the enterprise was to come from the founding insurance companies. On 1 January 1833 the LFEE came into existence, and James Braidwood accepted the post of superintendent.

Despite the professionalisation of the urban fire brigades in the 1820s and '30s, the architecture did not initially change, with the form of fire stations remaining similar to simple industrial buildings. The emphasis was still on the technologies, the appliances, equipment and response times. Firemen were usually still retained, so most stations were not residential and remained fairly small – one or two appliance bays with an office to one side, some store rooms beyond and not much more. The headquarters of the LFEE in Watling Street, City, included a mess room with kitchen for the men and a flat for the superintendent's family on the upper floors.

The mixture of privately funded brigades that existed gave many local authorities the excuse not to set up municipal brigades, which would require additional rates, bound to be unpopular. Rural locations retained the parish tradition of storing fire equipment in a simple, central shed, barn or other convenient position. For volunteer brigades that relied on members of the public, the fire engine house would be a great source of civic pride

Above: Fire at the Royal Exchange, London, 1838. The first Royal Exchange was destroyed in 1666 but rebuilt by Edward Jerman in 1669. This second building tragically burnt down in 1838. In this illustration, firemen can be seen directing water onto the fire from the street and from adjoining buildings, with cistern engines being pumped by volunteers and bucket chains refilling the cisterns.

Right: This proposed floor plan for an insurance fire brigade building shows a board room, dining room and offices upstairs, which are above an appliance bay, offices and stores on the ground floor. No accommodation for fire fighters is included, as at this time they would be retained.

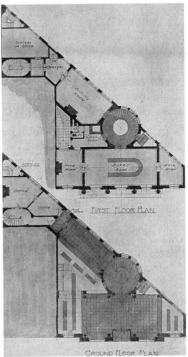

FIRST FLOOR PLAN

GROUND FLOOR PLAN

The storehouse, a traditional timber-framed barn with a large front porch in Newbury, Berkshire. This photograph taken in 1895 shows the fire station on the left-hand side – a brick building extension to the older agricultural group.

Ely, Cambridgeshire. The fire engine house is the building to the left-hand side, built alongside the adjacent residence in the mid-eighteenth century. Constructed in local stone and of simple, agricultural form, the building could have been used for a variety of activities; however, it housed the town's horse-drawn fire engine at the turn of the century. It was subsequently converted to a restaurant.

and, as such, they began to become more architecturally embellished, although commonly existing buildings were still adapted to house fire equipment. A typical example is the former fire station in Cobham, Kent. Originally constructed as a school house in 1839, the two buildings became redundant in 1861, when one building was adapted to provide an almshouse, the other becoming a parish hall and sometime soup kitchen. In 1890 the hall was again converted, by the insertion of a large door opening, to become a fire engine house, in which use it remained until a purpose-built fire station was erected for the town in the 1960s. This practicality in adapting existing structures typifies early fire engine houses, and means that, up until the mid-nineteenth century, fire stations were still not instantly identifiable from their architectural form as a distinct building type.

By the 1850s many insurance companies held the view that local authorities should contribute to the cost of providing a fire service, if not running that service themselves.

Newcastle was a major industrial city but had no municipal fire brigade – instead, it was protected by two insurance company brigades, the Newcastle-upon-Tyne Fire Office, with two fire engines, and the North British Insurance Company, with just one. Some large factories had their own to supplement coverage. Even a major fire in 1854 was not enough to force the Newcastle Corporation to take action. In 1866, upon receipt of notice that the North British Insurance Company intended to disband its brigade in the city and hand all equipment over to the authorities, the corporation was forced to broker a deal whereby the two insurance companies were combined as a new, municipal police-fire brigade.

Did you know?

Early fire brigades were not responsible for the protection of people, so the Royal Society for the Protection of Life from Fire was established in 1836. Its principal role was to place wheeled escape ladders in London streets to be used to save lives while the brigades arrested the spread of fire. The Royal Society was disbanded in 1866, with the equipment and the responsibility for saving lives from fire transferring to the newly created metropolitan fire brigade.

This pair of buildings in Cobham, Surrey, were originally a purpose-built school, constructed in 1839. From 1861 the right-hand building became an almshouse, with the left-hand building operating as a parish hall. In 1890 the hall was converted into a fire engine house, in which use it remained until the 1960s.

The invention of the steam-powered fire engine by Braithwaite in the 1830s, and the introduction of the first commercially successful version by Shand Mason in 1858, once again revolutionised the industry, replacing manual pumps. This was professional equipment that required professional operatives. For the first time, onlookers were being asked to step back, rather than to step up and help. This advancement really cemented the professional role of the fire fighter and from this point the buildings began to reflect this, moving away from mid-Victorian utility to more varied, richer designs that began to express the fire brigade through architecture.

It was yet another great fire that forced London to adopt a fully municipal fire brigade. On 22 June 1861 a fire broke out on the South Bank of the Thames and soon 1,000 yards of river frontage was aflame. As the fire raged out of control, Superintendent James Braidwood was killed by falling masonry. His body was not recovered for three days, and

Above: A coloured lithograph shows the severity of the great fire of Tooley Street, June 1861. To the right are London Bridge and the tower of Southwark Cathedral. Warehouses spread from here down to Tower Bridge, between the river and Tooley Street behind.
Left: Captain Eyre Massey Shaw. A cartoon from *Punch* magazine from 1891 showing Shaw with an MFB helmet and a steam fire engine in the background.

the Great Fire of Tooley Street was finally extinguished after two weeks. The estimated insurance bill for the companies involved in the LFEE (by now numbering thirty) was put at £2 million. Their premiums rocketed, causing complaints from policy holders across the country. Braidwood's replacement was recruited from the Belfast Brigade, Captain (later Sir) Eyre Massey Shaw. His dynamism matched that of Braidwood, and his political and royal connections helped to ensure that on 1 January 1866 the LFEE became a municipal fire service, changing its name to the Metropolitan Fire Brigade (MFB). Shaw proposed increasing from 129 firemen to 232 and nineteen stations to forty-three, thus embarking on the largest fire station building programme the UK has ever seen.

Did you know?

Baron, the Great Dane of Whitefriars Street station; Our Jim in Manchester; Wallace in Edinburgh; and Chance, the 1830s fire dog of Watling Street are just some of the famous pets adopted by brigades over the years. It was not just dogs that made suitable fire brigade pets – in 1906 *Chums Magazine for Boys* wrote to the LFB asking for a complete list of station pets, and received this official response: twelve dogs, three cats, two parrots and a cockatoo, two goats, one hedgehog and one squirrel!

This popular Victorian illustration of 1834 shows the famous canine mascot of the LFEE, Chance the fire dog, at the great fire of the palace of Westminster. The men of the LFEE awarded him a special collar inscribed, 'Stop me not but onward let me jog, For I am Chance the London Firemen's dog'.

5

Purpose-Built Fire Stations: The Golden Age

In the latter half of the nineteenth century Britain was still organised along mediaeval parish boundaries, with a large amount of power still held in vestries and local boards. The creation of new government structures, such as the Metropolitan Board of Works (MBW) in London in 1855, was an attempt to divest municipal authority with the powers to govern an area. Across the country rapidly expanding industrial towns like Manchester, Stoke-on-Trent, Newcastle and Glasgow needed to give substance to their new cities, with new city authorities and new institutions.

Off to the fire! A nineteenth-century London Fire Brigade illustration of a horse-drawn steam pump on a shout. The civilian driver of earlier illustrations has gone, replaced by a fireman, further professionalising the image of the brigade.

An early London station, Southwark Street SE1 of 1868 by Edward Cresy for the MFB – it was superseded in 1877 by the Southwark headquarters. This building is rather plain, although it has some decorative detail, but its scale and massing are common to mid-Victorian industrial buildings.

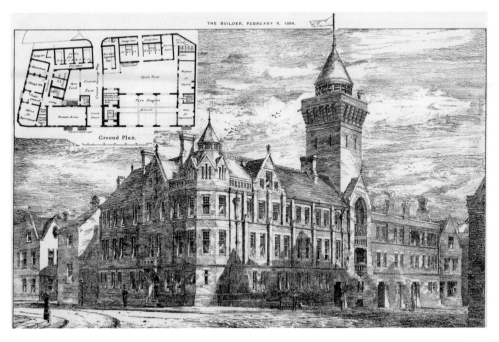

A proposal for a combined police and fire station headquarters for Newcastle by W. H. Seth-Smith, 1883. It was sadly never built. The plan shows bays for three appliances, an adjoining superintendent's office and stabling and stores to the rear of the yard. Adjacent to the stables is a hose store, and the area beneath the magnificent tower is noted as 'supplementary hose store'. A repair workshop is also included.

The ensuing building boom left a fine legacy of civic buildings: town halls, police stations, schools, hospitals and fire stations. The response to this demand for building was met by a generation of architects who found themselves faced with a series of questions on architectural identity. What was the appropriate architectural style for a fire station or a public wash house? Would they be the same in Dorking and Dundee? How could new ideas or technologies, or new places, be given a sense of stability and longevity through architecture? Various schools of thought on these subjects arose, and the ensuing debates became known as 'The Battle of the Styles'.

The debate centred initially on classical versus gothic architecture. The classical architecture of Greece and Rome implied the strength, stability and wisdom of ancient civilisations. This was a stolid architecture, strictly conforming to rules laid down centuries ago. It would lend an ancient and strong set of qualities to your new fire station or town hall, inspiring feelings of trustworthiness. It was not, however, traditionally British. This was the main criticism of proponents of the gothic school. Technically, gothic architecture was not British either, but it was assimilated as the defining architecture of Britain in the early mediaeval period, and was considered by many the more suitable style to express Britain's history. Again, it would link back to Britain's past and in so doing relate the brand new technical college, or town hall or indeed fire station, to emotive concepts of heritage, stability and reliability.

Above left: Shoreditch fire station, Tabernacle St, EC1 – built in 1895 by LCC architects on a tapering corner site, with originally three appliance bays on the end elevation, rising up with rounded corner towers and a highly decorative, rather delicate French-inspired roof form. Despite damage in the First World War, this station continued in use until 1964.

Above right: Manchester Square fire station (fondly referred to as 'the square'), of 1896 by Robert Pearsall for the LCC architects, highly articulated in a Tudor gothic style. Details include helmeted firemen-head corbels. The appliance bay doors were replaced in the 1960s to better allow for motorised vehicles. Closed in 2005.

Urban District Council fire station in Market Harborough, Leicestershire, of 1903 – it doubled in size in 1912 to a matching design. Original folding doors survive, along with green glazed brick and granite bases to the piers. A strong example of the English Free Style of architecture, practical and legibly civic.

A handsome former fire station of 1902 designed by the Urban Council Surveyor for Rushden, Northamptonshire. This was Rushden Fire Brigade's first purpose-built fire station since their formation in 1877. Although the decorative arched appliance bay doors have been lost, the fire station and attached cottage retain a strong presence.

Architects began to ruthlessly plunder elements from a variety of historical sources, and resultantly the early municipal fire stations are eclectic in style, although they tend to draw on established architectural languages and historical associations.

The MBW took over responsibility for designing new fire stations for London and, between 1867 and 1871, twenty-six new fire stations were built to the designs of Edward Cresy the Younger, succeeded by Alfred Mott and latterly Robert Pearsall. Cresy considered the appropriate style for fire stations to be 'Secular Gothick', a style that found continued favour with both Mott and Pearsall. A number of these early gothic MBW fire stations survive, now mostly converted to other uses.

The rigorous application of historical architectural languages began to soften, and architects found that they could draw on elements of particular styles and traditions, but update and adapt them. An interest in the honesty and quality of material and craftsmanship gave rise to the Arts and Crafts style. A freer hand in design, creatively combining elements of different traditional styles, gave rise to the emergence of the English Free Style, a new architecture of Englishness drawing strongly on vernacular architectural traditions, stylised and simplified for the new century. Early examples can be seen in model housing estates and schools, and particularly in fire stations. This fast became a favoured style for civic buildings.

Small substations and rural stations of the later Victorian period remained a garage structure to store the engine and equipment, but even these began to become more embellished. In rural areas they drew on vernacular architectural traditions, using local materials and decorative detailing, and often featured identifying details such as a small bellcote. For practical reasons, existing buildings also continued to be adapted.

For a medium-sized fire station in a town, a distinct building type housing the specialist functions of a fire brigade began to emerge in the 1840s and '50s. These would usually be built in brick with stone dressing, using hardwearing materials inside. Exposed brick and glazed brick wall finishes were common, as were hardwood blocks or stone sets for the appliance bay flooring. Entrance halls often featured hardwearing terrazzo floors. Plain, robust concrete stairs with very simple, unadorned cast-iron stick balusters were standard. Fire station interiors were generally fairly practical, utilitarian spaces.

As brigades became increasingly professional, they began to keep their own horses. While commonly still rented from commercial stables, horses were now kept at the fire stations in teams, and the stations increased in size to include permanent stabling. The layout expanded to include stable bays, behind the appliance bays. The floor inside the appliance bay would often include a sloping section leading down towards the doors, which would assist the horses to get the fire engines rolling faster as they left the station. So, as the horses went through the doors, they were already 'on the run', a phrase that is still used by fire fighters today to mean 'ready for action'. If something is 'off the run', it is out of order.

The small, green timber building here is a substation established in St Enoch's Square, Glasgow, in the 1890s. It had a staff of three men and, as well as a fire cart, it had a 50-foot wheeled escape ladder, which can just be made out on the right-hand side.

Above left: The Chippenham Yelde Hall in Wiltshire is an early fifteenth-century building that has served a wide range of uses during its lifetime. In 1910 major structural adaptations were made, and the present double doors inserted, to enable its use as a fire station. It remained in this use until 1945. It now houses a museum.

Above right: Detail of a glazed brick arch at the former fire station in Belsize, London. The ceiling to the appliance bay beyond demonstrates how a practical approach has been taken to routing services.

Right: Substation in Asfordby Street, Leicester, built 1899 with the adjacent police station by Arthur Wakerley. While simple in form, the building is decorated with brickwork, banded stone and an oculus window, affording a distinguished appearance and showing the pride taken in the local fire brigade. Closed in 1973.

A critically important space within any fire station was the watch room, where the call would be received and which included accommodation for the duty officer. The watch room and station office would overlook the appliance bays, located to one side of them.

The practice yard to the rear served a number of important functions, providing space for drills and equipment inspection, for wash-down and for laying-out, drying and repairing hoses. Hoses would need to be hung out to dry, and so winching hooks would be provided, either on a sheltered external elevation in the yard, or else often within the stairwell of the fire station. The yard would include a return by means of a back gate (horses could not be reversed, and so would need to be returned via a different route to line up efficiently facing outwards again for the next shout). Storage for coal, hay and fodder would be arranged around the yard. Storage for more specialist equipment, including a kit room, would be located communicating with the appliance bays. On upper floors, a mess room or recreation room would usually be provided, adjacent to a kitchen.

Medium to large fire stations would feature a fire lamp on the front. This was once a very standard feature, and would be affixed to the external elevation or positioned on a stone gate or railing pier. Since these have fallen from use, many have been lost, and surviving fire lamps on buildings become rarer. Designs vary across the country; early London fire lamps feature dark-blue glass with white lettering – later, fire authorities used red glass.

Larger brigades with full-time firemen provided similar accommodation on the ground floor to that described above, with residential accommodation on the upper floors, requiring the largest buildings. Recruitment of ex-sailors was still favoured; these were men used to dangerous working conditions, agile when working at heights and with ropes, used to an all-hands-on-deck on-call mentality and to hierarchy and obeying orders – ideal for the new professional brigades. Sailors were also used to restricted living conditions. Brigades provided

Fenton, Staffordshire. Purpose-built fire station of 1909/10. Fenton retained its own fire brigade until the reorganisation of Stoke-on-Trent fire service in 1926, when this building fell out of use. A strong and robust industrial building with a decorative tower, it is instantly recognisable as a fire station.

MFB fire station at Roman Road, London, of 1888 by architect Alfred Mott for the Metropolitan Board of Works. A large, solid and confident building in the style of Norman Shaw, its decorative brick and stonework highlight the appliance bays and the sexagonal corner tower, part of the richly embellished roofline.

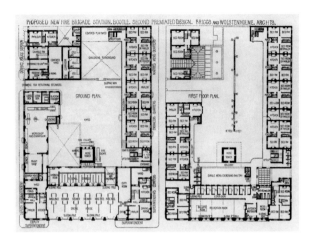

Floor plan of a proposed fire station for Bolton, Manchester, 1899. The appliance bay has room for three steamers, two hose reels and an ambulance. Sliding poles lead from the recreation room to the appliance bays. This plan shows the type of frugal accommodation firemen were offered on site, including single men's cubicles and exercising balcony. The superintendent's quarters are more generously laid out over two floors.

dormitories for unmarried men in addition to a mess room, together with a kitchen. Spartan accommodation for married quarters was provided in the form of small flats of one or two bedrooms, with a living room and scullery. Larger stations would keep more horses, and had some extra stabling off the yard for horses not 'on call'. Separate accommodation for a groom to care for the horses or for coachmen was usually included above the stables, accessed separately from the yard. Another common feature of larger stations was an on-site workshop for the repair of appliances and equipment. This would be a relatively plain building, usually located to the rear of the yard. Some two-storey workshops were built, although in modern times workshops have often been demolished to increase the size of the yard for car parking.

Extra residential accommodation was often built or privately rented nearby. Sometimes, groups of firemen's cottages survive to the rear of fire stations. These tend to be of standard design for residential accommodation, without any specific adaptation to indicate that they were built specifically for firemen. Superintendents were expected to live on site above the fire station, although they and their families would be afforded more generous living quarters; this was often still a flat within the building, but were of grander proportions and likely to have its own front doors.

The entire community within a fire station would be subject to a curfew – and, for this reason, the main residential entrance door for accessing the upper floors was usually located next to the watch room, or else the only exit was through the appliance bay, so that all movements could be monitored from a single position. Communal laundries were common within larger stations, and were located in the basement, off the yard, or occasionally, such as at Clerkenwell or London Road, Manchester, in the attic storey.

Many larger stations included a panelled billiards room for recreation, usually featuring built-in seating and storage for billiard cues within the panelling. Sometimes, such as at Rochdale, the recreation room is even grander, located above the appliance bay and presented as a ballroom with a stage at one end, intended for wider community use.

Bigger station buildings meant that it took more time to assemble the crew when the shout came in. An American invention, the sliding pole allowed for quicker access to the appliance bay from the upper floors. These were introduced and very quickly adopted, fast becoming a symbolic element of the fire station. Due to the risks of creating the required opening in the floor, pole housing in the form of panelled timber dividers with a quick-release door would

Did you know?

The fireman's pole was invented by Captain David Kenyon, a fireman in Chicago in 1878, and was first made of pine, coated in varnish and paraffin. This was soon replaced with brass.

usually encase the pole-drop. Poles were introduced to London fire stations after a 1904 fact-finding trip to New York. These were not the first in the country, however. Architectural plans for Rawtenstall fire station in Lancashire, built in 1897, include a pair of poles.

From the late nineteenth century onwards, fire stations, particularly in urban areas, tend to utilise a balcony access arrangement on the rear elevation, allowing separate entrances for the flats located above the station – an arrangement that remained popular for residential buildings well into the late twentieth century. The benefit of these open balconies at a fire station is that they allow you to see and hear what is happening in the yard even from upper floors. The London Fire Brigade's 1937 headquarters at Albert Embankment by E. P. Wheeler feature eight stories of balconies on the rear elevation; the lower balconies extend out and were intended to be used as display platforms for up to 800 people to watch weekly public drill displays.

The continuous drive to improve efficiency through response times meant that fire stations continued to accommodate new and revolutionary technologies. The automatic horse harness would use pulleys to lower the harnesses onto the horse's back as soon as the call came in. Pulley systems also enabled the stalls and appliance bay doors to be swung open automatically. The

Interior of the fire station at Port Sunlight, designed 1902 by William Owen for Lever Bros' soap works to provide cover to their factory as well as to the model village of workers' cottages built on the Wirral. Firefighting equipment and fire fighters' coats and helmets can be seen.

introduction of the telegraph system enabled calls to reach the fire station much more quickly, and meant the introduction of specialist telephonic equipment into the watch room or station office.

As the role and equipment of fire brigades rapidly developed, so it was not uncommon for a fire station of the 1850s to have been superseded before 1900 with a larger, more specialised station. One thing that was resisted by the London Brigade was the inclusion on their appliances of bells to sound as they raced through the streets, which they feared would spook the horses. Instead they were famous for the cry 'Hi! Yi!' as noted in the diary of the writer and newspaper editor R. D. Blumenfeld, 1901:

> The fire brigade came dashing down the Strand at Wellington Street to-day with the usual wild cries of 'Hi! yi! hi! yi!' which always creates a sensation in the streets ...

Did you know?

In the Victorian period, it was commonly said that, while their ladders were made of wood, the firemen's hearts were made of steel.

Illustrations of the Grand Meet of Fire Brigades in Oxford, 1887. The university organised a part-time fire service which remained active until the 1880s. A volunteer brigade was established in 1870, rivalled by the police fire brigade from 1871. The volunteer brigade remained active until 1940, when it came under the control of the city corporation. The illustration shows the great pride and public interest taken in fire brigades in the late Victorian period.

The suggestion so often made that the firemen should abandon their wild and alarming cries and substitute a gong is bitterly opposed by the firemen. They have always yelled 'Hi! yi!' and they always will do so.

Fire brigades espoused reliability and bravery in the Victorian psyche, and this fed perfectly into the romantic image that the fireman took on in Victorian art. The swooning lady in a white nightdress being carried to safety over the shoulder of the strong, uniformed fireman amid smoke and danger became a defining image of the period. With images such as this in the Victorian mind, confidence was the order of the day for fire

Left: The men of the Manchester Fire Brigade pose for the camera, showing literally the lengths they can go to for your safety. Three men stand on each section of the extending ladders. Taken at Albert Square, Manchester; undated.
Below: Police and fire station, London Road, Manchester, 1901–6. It has red brick liberally decorated with terracotta, including statues and relief panels, and is arranged around a central courtyard, with the appliance bays (for seven vehicles) and stalls (for fourteen horses) fronting out onto Fairfield Street.

Whitworth Street, Fire Station and Public Offices, Manchester

brigades, as seen in the public displays and drills, their impression upon the media of the time, and also in the architectural confidence of fire stations.

The newly civic fire stations became the responsibility of the local authorities, and so were commonly designed by the borough architects. Finding an individual architect's name associated with a fire station can be difficult for this reason, as they're often attributed to 'the borough architect', or similar. The largest city fire stations would be subject to architectural competitions.

A state-of-the-art central fire station, combined with police station, magistrates' court and electricity test house, was built at London Road, Manchester, between 1901 and 1906 by architects Woodhouse, Willoughby & Langham. This three-sided building ranged around a courtyard was greatly lauded at the time of its completion. The confident Edwardian baroque style was selected to hark back to the architecture of Sir Christopher Wren 200 years earlier. The building's external elevations abound in decorative embellishment: terracotta panels, swags, projecting balconies and allegorical sculpture. The complexity of plan form, the exterior and interior decoration (particularly in the watch room), and the sheer size, scale and prominence of this building typify the turn-of-the-century attitude towards fire stations. The design not only imbues the fire station with the historical association of the English Baroque, but the might of the building and its wealth of decoration also suggest positive ideas about the wealth, status and importance of the brigade.

The rear elevation of the fire station in Barry, South Wales, built 1901. The building uses French and Italianate architectural references, culminating in the extraordinary practice tower with copper pavilion roof, an instant local landmark.

A detail showing the six-stage hose-drying tower at Leicester central station, 1925–7. The striking tower has a variety of balconies on its exterior, and at the top a clock face on each side.

The architectural manifestation of pride in fire station design is summed up in the watch tower.

So many fire stations included towers, and they served a highly practical purpose. The hoses of the Victorian period required hanging out to dry after each use, and so a tall, narrow space such as the inside of a tower was perfect for this. Commonly on architectural plans these towers are described as hose-drying towers. However, in the popular imagination they are watch towers, from where, much like the masts of old ships, firemen kept watch, and you will find that atop these towers there are walkways, balconies and look-outs. References to and illustrations of firemen actually keeping watch from the top of towers can be found in newspaper and magazine accounts of the time. The idea that, amid all the smoking chimneys of an industrial town, a fire would be spotted from such a distance and the engines dispatched accordingly seems extraordinarily unlikely. Far more practical, as well as hose drying, is the idea that the towers helped to forge a distinctly recognisable building type, and shaped fire stations' identity as civic buildings. The tower has become a ubiquitous part of the fire station, although today the purpose of the tower is firmly for training.

At the turn of the twentieth century, fire brigades were at the forefront of technological innovation, firemen having become a symbol of heroism and the fire station being a source of civic pride to every town. Many stations and substations were built in this period and, while the provision and plan form stayed essentially the same, an astonishing variety of architectural solutions was found to embody the fire brigade.

Did you know?

Edward, Prince of Wales, later Edward VII, was an amateur fire brigade enthusiast, rumoured to have kept his own uniform ready at Chandos Street fire station at all times and to actually have attended several major London fires, masquerading as an ordinary member of the brigade.

The city fire engine of Lincoln resided in this purpose-built engine house of 1880, which also bears the Mayor's name and crest. It adjoins the city police station, and shows some architectural distinction through decorative brickwork.

This was the first purpose-built fire station in Wolverhampton, West Midlands, built contingent with the town hall in 1871 and using architectural detailing to represent pride in the town authority. The brigade in Wolverhampton had been established in 1855. The building remained in use until the 1960s.

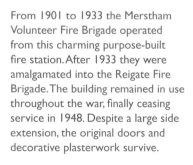

From 1901 to 1933 the Merstham Volunteer Fire Brigade operated from this charming purpose-built fire station. After 1933 they were amalgamated into the Reigate Fire Brigade. The building remained in use throughout the war, finally ceasing service in 1948. Despite a large side extension, the original doors and decorative plasterwork survive.

Left: Malvern Wells fire station in Worcestershire was originally built in 1897 and is a proud little Victorian fire station, using good quality local materials with some architectural embellishment to demark its civic function. It appears to have decommissioned by the time of the Second World War, and then brought back into use under the NFS before finally closing a second time in 1945.

Below: Westminster fire station, 1906, by the LCC architects' department. It is of the English Free Style with baroque references, particularly in the brick pilasters and Ionic capitals. This shows clever modelling of a difficult site; note that the end elevation originally features an additional appliance bay.

Above: Clerkenwell fire station by H. F. T. Cooper for the LCC architects' department. The 1870s station was extended in 1896 and replaced by this building in 1911–13. The two right-hand bays incorporate the 1896 extension; the 1870 building was pulled down, showing the rapidly changing requirements from urban fire stations, with three stations in just forty years. Clerkenwell was closed in 2009.

Below: Two uniformed firemen pose ready with a steam fire engine outside Blenheim palace in Oxfordshire in the 1870s. Many country houses and estates had their own fire equipment. This one is decorated with the name Blenheim. The men hold copper nozzles to attach to the reeled hoses on the appliance.

Left: Hungerford Weathervane, a decorative weathervane with 'HVFB' for Hungerford Volunteer Fire Brigade, Berkshire, showing the pride taken in volunteer fire brigades. The HVFB began in 1891 and was one of the last purely volunteer-based fire brigades in the country.

Below: Lauriston Place fire station, Edinburgh, headquarters of the Edinburgh Fire Brigade from its construction in 1897 until 1988. Designed by Robert Mortham in the Queen Anne style and built in red sandstone with granite demarking the appliance bays, until recently it has housed the Museum of the Lothian and Borders Fire Brigade.

6

Twentieth Century: Wartime Firefighting

At the beginning of the twentieth century, fire station design once again had to adapt to technological changes. The internal combustion engine, introduced shortly after the turn of the century, was increasingly used to drive the appliance and pump the water. In 1905 the first London fire station to be built entirely for motorised appliances was completed at Red Lion Street in Wapping. This was the beginning of the end for the brigade's long reliance on horses, and earlier stations, with stables, returns and stores for hay and fodder, now required adaptation.

Motorised equipment was introduced to many pre-existing stations, requiring the appliance bay doors to be enlarged and stable-boxes, automatic harnesses and other equipment relating to horses to be stripped out of appliance bays. Radiators were often put in between the bays at this time – not for the benefit of the firemen, but for the engines, as early engines needed to be kept warm in order for them to start properly. The introduction of central heating for this purpose meant that the upper floors could also be heated efficiently, enabling the removal of coal fires and fireplaces from the residential accommodation. In many cases the reordering required to adapt a fire station from horse-drawn to motorised appliances would have been so substantial that it was considered more efficient to relocate the fire station entirely. In densely built city centres, this often meant the demolition of the earlier station and its replacement with a new building on the same site.

Old-fashioned equipment continued in use after the First World War, however. On 21 November 1921 London's last fire horses, 'brigade greys' called Lucy and Nora, turned out of Kensington fire station.

The Fire Brigades Union came into existence in 1918, and has been continuously involved in improving conditions for fire fighters ever since.

HM Dockyard fire station, Portsmouth, Hampshire. The cast-iron structure of 1843 supports a large water tank above the appliance bays. Firemen pose on fire engines, up ladders and, seen in the centre, modelling early breathing apparatus. This dockyard fire station is one of the earliest examples of the use of corrugated-iron cladding panels. Photographed c. 1900.

In the early 1920s another change came about with the introduction of the watch system, in which fire fighters work shifts. This moved away from professional firemen being continuously on call and living at the fire station, introduced better working conditions for professional firemen and meant that fire stations required less residential accommodation, meaning they could become smaller buildings once again.

Larger headquarters retained the upper floors, with a mixture of office and sleeping accommodation. The heart of the fire station remained the watch room, strategically adjacent to and overlooking the appliance bays. The mess room and kitchen also remained of central importance.

Improvements to breathing apparatus meant that this equipment required its own distinct space within a fire station, with cleanable surfaces and a sink for hot water, kept separate from oil and other such substances. A breathing apparatus room or BA room was included in the limited stations that had BA equipment up until the late 1930s.

Victorian stations, designed with hierarchical accommodation, communal laundries, and laid out for stables and horse-drawn appliances, became not only functionally redundant, but, with all their gothic or Queen Anne detailing, also stylistically fell out of fashion. The sleek style of the 1930s marked a cultural shift away from the busy architecture of the previous generations.

Many large and small fire stations of the 1930s, including those in Northampton, 1935, Bridgend, 1936, and Dunstable, Bedfordshire, 1939, were built entirely for mechanised appliances, and with a watch system of staffing in mind. Using modern materials these stations encapsulate the progressive mood of the period and express the rapid technological development that was reshaping the fire service.

Reacting against the efficiency and modernity of architecture at this time, some architects preferred to work in the neo-classical language. The headquarters at Leicester, 1927, and the fire station at Harrow, London, from 1937 both use familiar, domestic architectural form.

The development of the fully enclosed 'limousine' pump made for a safer, more sheltered journey from the station to the site of the fire. Edinburgh first introduced such a vehicle (a Merryweather) in 1931 amid criticism from older members of the brigade that protecting firemen in this way was pampering. The first limousine pumps introduced to London were built and delivered by Dennis in 1935. Again, some senior firemen considered this mollycoddling. Despite these advances, open-bodied fire engines remained in common use across the country until the late 1950s. The dual-purpose appliance, with both a pump and ladder, was introduced in 1934.

The Mounts fire station was built as headquarters to the Northampton Fire Brigade in 1935, as they switched to motorised vehicles and relocated from a narrow town centre back street to a grander location, with all the architectural confidence of the period. This is one of the 1930s super stations.

A stylish but modest building using classical Doric columns in a restrained Art Deco design. Derwent Street, Bridgend, South Wales. Of unknown origin, it is recorded as a fire station in the 1950s, and was subsequently used as a post office depot. Currently vacant.

This simple but elegant fire station was built in 1939 in Dunstable, Bedfordshire. Replaced with a much larger station in 1965, it was then used as an ambulance depot, and currently as a youth centre. Art Deco stylings alleviate a plain, rectangular form.

Leicester Central fire station, 1925–7, by A. & T. Sawday. A symmetrical and polite neo-Georgian design with eight appliance bays, offices and a recreational hall over. The domestic brick walls and pantile roof dress a steel-framed building behind.

Harrow fire station, London, of 1937 in a domestic revival style, but with the three appliance bay doors framed and highlighted by stone surrounds. Formerly Middlesex Fire Brigade, the building was transferred to the London Fire Brigade in 1965, when it had eighteen firemen. It remains in active use.

The old fire station in Uckfield, East Sussex, served from 1937 to 1996. A confident civic design in traditional brickwork, symmetrical with linked cottages either side, three appliance bays with mess room over. The centre bay rises up to a raised pediment featuring a clock. A striking building.

A motorised limousine fire engine supplied to the Edinburgh Fire Brigade by Dennis Bros in 1932. The first engine of this style was supplied to Edinburgh in 1931, and was clearly considered a success as this one was supplied just one year later.

Private industrial sites such as the Kodak factory in Harrow, London, and the Boots factory in Beeston, Nottinghamshire, continued to erect and maintain their own fire stations into the mid-twentieth century, alongside municipal brigades. This was based on the increased risk of fire at industrial sites, the same reason that military sites and, increasingly, airports would build their own fire stations. These tend to be simpler than municipal fire stations, consisting of appliance bays with an office and stores to one side. They do not require residential accommodation, relying on retained members of the existing work force instead. Despite their being a simple place to store equipment rather

The New Rowntree Cocoa Works fire engine, supplied by Merriweather, at the Rowntree factory in York, Yorkshire, 1929. An example of a private fire brigade employed directly by a factory owner due to the increased risk such sites possessed.

Purpose-built fire station at the Boots Wet Processes factory, Beeston, Nottinghamshire, of 1938 by Evan Owen Williams. With its reinforced concrete frame and expressed cantilevers, this building was at the forefront of technology when built.

than a fully functioning fire station as we would understand it, the private fire stations of industrial sites often use progressive or experimental architectural form and materials, as seen at Beeston, which included a striking practice tower. Military sites and airports tend to treat their fire stations in a more utilitarian manner.

In the late 1930s the political situation across Europe was heighted by the threat of war. Aerial bombardment of British cities and industries was becoming an increasingly real and terrifying prospect. Major industrial centres such as the docks in Southampton, Cardiff, Liverpool and London, as well as coastal and manufacturing towns, posed significant fire risks with residential populations in densely packed housing adjacent to major targets.

A review of resilience to fire, particularly to aerial attack, led to the adoption in January 1938 of the Air Raid Precautions Act. This established a central government grant to fund improvements to firefighting services, which included the formation of an Auxiliary Fire Service of volunteers. The AFS was already underway recruiting and training volunteers before the announcement of war in September 1939. Many professional firemen had been called up to military service, so the men and women who put themselves forward to join the fire brigades, either full or part time, were vital in filling this gap.

This was the first admission of women into the fire service, although they were permitted only to take up administrative roles, or to be drivers. They played vital roles, and many AFS women demonstrated significant bravery throughout the war years.

New substations, appliances and equipment were urgently required and across Britain AFS substations were either hastily erected temporary buildings or requisitioned sites such as drill halls, schools, garages or industrial buildings. This Kentish AFS brigade is operating a substation from a caravan. On Merseyside, by 1941, Liverpool had 132 AFS stations; Hoylake and West Kirby had eight; Southport seven; the Wirral five; Huyton-with-Roby two; and Formby just one.

January 1940. AFS men at work on their trailer pump outside the Northfleet substation in Kent. The substation is a caravan covered in tin sheeting, canvas and sand bags. This makeshift approach typifies many early AFS substations.

Right: Female volunteers of the AFS resting in makeshift bunks in the basement of the London Fire Brigade headquarters, Albert Embankment, during the Second World War.
Below: This building in Heathfield, East Sussex, was in use as a fire station prior to 1931, and was used by the AFS during the war. Hastily built and simple in form and material, it has survived adapted for various uses.

In some cases off-duty AFS staff with peacetime careers in construction erected purpose-built stations. These are characterised by their economy and simplicity, as might be expected in this period. Emergency water pipelines and dams (containers) were set up in locations that were either considered high risk or far from natural water sources. New fire engines were ordered, finished in austere gun-metal grey. Even a fleet of 2,000 taxi cabs was requisitioned in London, coupled to trailers fitted-up for use by the AFS.

Did you know?

Up until 1938 the responsibility for local authorities to provide a fire brigade remained discretionary, so volunteer brigades continued to operate. Compulsory provision was only achieved by the creation of the Auxiliary Fire Service in anticipation of the Second World War.

Before the outbreak of war Britain had over 1,600 fire brigades. By 1939 almost all had a separate AFS attachment but standardisation across the service was proving difficult to co-ordinate. By November 1940, with continual bombing every night for over a month in the London Blitz, enemy attacks began to spread across the country. Birmingham, Bristol, Coventry, Liverpool and Southampton were targets. By December, Sheffield and Manchester had also been hit and London was receiving another hammering. This led the Home Office to establish the National Fire Service (NFS) in 1941.

Legislation centralised command and divided the country into eleven regions, subdivided into thirty-three fire force areas. All of the personnel, engines and equipment of the brigades and the AFS were transferred, and a national chain of command was established. New uniforms, badges, insignia and training manuals were distributed.

A purpose-built NFS substation in district 34, Bushey, Hertfordshire, 1942. With lulls in the enemy action over London, fire service personnel were put to more productive work using the skills they brought with them into the NFS.

An illustration showing one of 2,000 taxis that were fitted with a light trailer fire pump for the AFS, used to augment provision by the London Fire Brigade in 1938.

The NFS was taking shape at a moment when the German air force, the Luftwaffe, was shifting its focus to the Russian front, with a slight cessation in the intensity of bombing over the UK; however the 'Baedeker' raids of 1942, affecting Exeter, Bath, Norwich, York and Canterbury, caused considerable damage and tested the NFS across the country.

Once hostilities were finally over in 1945, the Home Office began to restore the now-nationalised fire service back to its pre-war arrangements. The Fire Services Act of 1948 placed the responsibility for maintaining efficient fire brigades with county or borough councils, creating 148 fire brigades across the UK. The NFS was gradually disbanded, and requisitioned buildings (where they had survived) were returned to their former uses. Nationally fire services began to take stock of their reduced personnel, war-damaged buildings and worn-out equipment.

During a training exercise, one fireman of the LFB descends from the drill tower towards a jumping sheet held by his colleagues below. The jumping sheet was a commonly used form of escape.

7
The Modern Fire Station

Whilst post-war Britain's attitude to the architecture of rebuilding was forward-thinking rebuilding battered Britain took time. Through the 1950s and '60s a wave of modern fire stations appeared. Cultural changes towards a post-industrial economy, increasing car ownership, increased reliance on central heating and electricity, and a host of other factors were changing the type of service and response required from the fire brigade, and therefore the type and location of fire stations. Larger suburbs and better road connections meant that, while some older inner city stations remained in use, modern stations could be located on new, more generous out-of-town sites with good connectivity to the road network.

Local authority capital-building programmes saw increasing standardisation in the construction of civic buildings. Schools, police and fire stations were using prefabricated building systems that could be rolled out across a region. Steel frames, concrete and prefabricated cladding panels, commonly featuring the use of asbestos, became more

View of former fire station, building 66 (foreground) at RAF Barnham in Suffolk. RAF Barnham was a special storage site for Britain's cold war bomber command. Given this use, a fire station was paramount and in 1958 the RAF fire service was located here. Buildings were constructed of steel and reinforced concrete.

Swindon, Wiltshire, from 1959 to present. Four appliance bays and a commanding central tower feature. The full height glazing to the right-hand side is a modern replacement of the original slender concrete glazing bars.

A three-bay fire station, built 1956, in Crawley, West Sussex, with watch room, entrance and accommodation to the right-hand side, and an unusual training tower to the rear. With decorative brickwork and featuring a bow-fronted window to the watch room.

Angel Street: a 1964 five-bay fire station with watch room and offices to the left and a training tower beyond at Angel Street, Bridgend, South Wales. The simple form of this building type is recognisable across the country.

This strongly industrial fire station in Blaina, Monmouthshire, dates from 1960. The tin cladding panels extend to the training tower, at the rear. Notice that the left-hand side of the building has subsequently become a café.

widespread, replacing masonry construction and decorative ornamentation with straight lines and geometric shapes redolent of the modernist aesthetic. Whether this was driven more by cost or style is debatable. Fire stations from the 1960s often therefore look fairly similar from one county to the next. What this does help to achieve is something that was of great concern to the Victorian architects: a strongly identifiable building type. A simple steel or concrete framed building – with the ubiquitous large red doors in front of a forecourt, a watch room and office to one side, a covered wash-down space and training tower behind – was universal.

Improvements to breathing apparatus equipment post-war soon meant that breathing apparatus became standard-issue kit at all fire stations. From the 1950s onwards stations included a BA room as standard. A mess room and kitchen were still included and, for larger stations, also dormitories or individual rooms for sleeping and showers. Increasingly, exercise equipment would be provided for firemen, and so throughout the twentieth century a gym became a typical space to find within a fire station. Older stations were often adapted to provide this, so it is common to find a gym created by subdividing the appliance bay, knocking together some smaller basement rooms, or other similar adaptations.

Larger appliances required larger appliance bays and larger doors. This adaptation is often prominent on older fire stations, where original brick arches have been replaced by straight steel or concrete lintels, and original brick piers between the appliance bay doors have been reduced or removed to allow larger equipment unimpeded access. (See image of Manchester Square fire station, pg 28) Purpose-built stations from this period onward tend to pre-empt the issue by incorporating large appliance bay doors.

Shoreditch fire station, a divisional headquarters built in 1964 to replace the 1895 station across the street. LCC architects' department. This is a confident design that echoes traditional fire station arrangements, with the six prominent appliance bays, projected watch room to the left and projected mess room above right. The accommodation over includes maisonettes with balconies on the top two floors, forming a striking architectural rhythm.

Oxford fire station, 1971. A strongly expressed structural frame defines both appliance bays and the three-storey training and accommodation building beyond. Prefabricated panels and brickwork alternate, and the appliance bay has set-back clerestory windows. A stripped-back training tower completes the group to the rear.

Interior view of the operations room of the central fire station, Hatton Garden, Liverpool, which was the principal station for Liverpool from its construction in 1897 to its closure in 1982. This 1970s equipment was once the height of technology.

A few outstanding fire stations of the later twentieth century survive, such as the divisional headquarters at Shoreditch, London, built in 1965 by LCC architects' department, and the Rewley Road fire station at Oxford, built in 1971. Headquarter buildings are typically of greater architectural merit than smaller stations and substations. As many towns had their headquarters rebuilt for petrol vehicles in the 1930s, they tend to have remained fit for purpose. These robust buildings have been able to accommodate adaptation, particularly for updated equipment in the watch room.

From the mid-twentieth century fire stations move away from multi-storied buildings towards laterally arranged plan forms, often single-storey, sometimes with a partial first floor. The reasons for this are many: improving turnout time being the foremost, while the move-to-watch system meant less residential accommodation was required; the shift from urban to suburban locations meant space was at less of a premium, and the famous fireman's pole, which had enabled quick response times in tall, many-storied fire stations, slipped out of favour as it became apparent that the amount of twisted ankles and other injuries caused by the poles were not outweighed by the time they saved. For all of these reasons, the standard form of the twentieth-century fire station commonly centres on the appliance bay, with the watch room, station office, BA and kit rooms opening off it, and additional staff accommodation above this, accessed by stairs. The covered wash-down area required at the rear in the yard usually took the form of a projecting, glazed canopy.

A large fire station from the mid-1970s in Merthyr, Mid Glamorgan. Using characteristic industrial materials of black brick and aluminium cladding, with watch room and offices to the right of the five appliance bays, and communal facilities to the left. A brick training tower appears beyond.

An unusual design for Allendale fire station, Northumberland, of the mid-1970s. The abstracted asymmetrical roofs separate out the central appliance bay, with the stores to the right and the watch room and accommodation to the left.

In 1974, local authority restructuring led to the amalgamation of a number of city and county fire brigades. This led to the building of more new fire stations, although the basic style, form, layout and materials of fire station construction did not significantly change.

The first fire authority to admit women to the role of fire fighter was the Grampian fire authority in Scotland in 1978. The first female fire fighter appointment in London was in 1982. Since this time the role and recognition of women fire fighters has substantively increased, and the buildings have had to adapt to accommodate this change. Originally designed only for male fire fighters, all fire stations have had to allow for female toilets, showers and changing facilities. In modern stations this has been relatively easy to achieve by adapting internal walls and reorganising facilities. In older stations, especially in listed stations, providing additional facilities in this way has been more challenging.

The creation of municipal boroughs in 1986 saw further restructuring to brigades. More recently, brigades have been moved from local authority control to become independent fire authorities. During this period, many older stations have been deemed redundant, either because of their internal configuration, the difficulties of adaptation or because of their location. A process of disposal of older fire stations, no longer fit for purpose, and their replacement with modern purpose-built stations continues. Finding Victorian fire stations that remain in active use is now quite difficult. Fulham fire station, London, built in 1895/6, is possibly the oldest active purpose-built fire station in the country; while the Old Harlow fire station of 1870 is an older active station, it was not purpose built and did not become a fire station until 1955.

Above: Dating from 1989, Market Harborough fire station in Leicestershire uses the traditional forms of fire station design gently stretched and subverted to post-modern shapes. The circular window is reminiscent of a number of Victorian stations, but the scale, with three appliance bays, is bigger here.
Below: Chippenham fire station of 1974 by Wiltshire County Council architects' department. An unusual inverted roof form, allowing a recreation room to fit over part of the appliance bay and the office, accommodation and storage to be housed in the building to the left-hand side.

Malvern fire station in Worcestershire dates from 2014 and replaces an earlier station on the same site. The straight lines and economy of design highlight the functionality of the four red appliance bay doors.

Middlesbrough community fire station, 2015, replaced an earlier station of 1939 but it was decided to retain and reuse the Venetian clock tower, proving how iconic the tower is to the identity of a fire station. The modern building uses red cladding to frame the appliance bay doors, echoing the stonework of earlier stations.

The changing role of the fire brigade has also seen a shift in emphasis towards the prevention of fire. This includes greater levels of education and community outreach, and taking a proactive role in community fire safety – engaging with the community, particularly inviting people into the fire station, as well as visiting schools, workplaces and homes. The resultant requirement for an education or community facility within the fire station means that these days it is common to find a multi-purpose community or training room incorporated into the fire station. Having members of the public on site also means the need for a 'front' and 'back of house' split – the resultant security issues can impact on fire station design.

Did you know?

Fire station doors have been redesigned over the years to achieve faster turnout times. Brigades currently tend to use four-fold side-motion doors that open approximately twice as fast as conventional rolling or sectional-overhead doors. Whilst the technology has advanced, the characteristic red colour for the doors has remained.

Many earlier fire stations have been decommissioned, sold, and then either demolished or adapted for alternative uses. Pre-war stations are very often listed for their special architectural or historic interest. As robustly constructed buildings with a range of larger and smaller spaces inside, they generally convert very well to alternative uses. Victorian stations tend to be in town centre locations, so the ground floor can find a new life as a commercial premises, bar or restaurant without the requirement to subdivide the appliance bay, replace the main doors or remove much of the characteristic detailing. Upper floors that were originally laid out for residential use can often fairly easily continue for that purpose without requiring significant adaptation. Fire stations make fairly good community centres or theatres, with numerous examples across the country, from Oxford to Dunfermline. Given the robust nature typical of fire stations, they also convert well to light industrial uses such as workshops or garages. The former station in Loughborough, Leicestershire, is successfully reused as a tyre-fitter.

At present there are sixty-three brigades covering England, Wales, Scotland and Northern Ireland. Modern stations are efficient and industrial in their materials and spatial qualities. Although fire stations no longer use such monumental architecture to announce their presence, they have achieved instant recognition through their architectural form, and are readily identifiable, respected civic buildings across the country.

Marley Park fire station, Sunderland, Tyne and Wear. Opened 2015. The materials are modern industrial, and the generous scale means this building is unmistakably civic.

8
What Now?

There are many ways to engage with both modern fire brigades and interest groups for fire brigade history. A range of specialist publications and websites offer further information, and a number of museums act as the focus for volunteer groups, open days and more.

Your local Fire and Rescue Service strives to be a strong part of the community. You will find them represented at community events and they are always happy to talk to you. They may well run open days and community activities at your local fire station, and usually offer a free home safety check service. All Fire and Rescue services have an online presence, through their websites and social media.

If you are researching particular building, you should first check whether it is listed. The National Heritage List for England (historicengland.org.uk/listing/the-list), the Heritage portal for Scotland (portal.historicenvironment.scot) and CADW in Wales (cadw.gov.wales/historicenvironment) will be the first port of call.

If you are caring for a decommissioned fire station, you will be able to get advice and guidance from the relevant amenity society. Contact the Victorian Society (020 8994 1019; www.victoriansociety.org.uk) or the Twentieth Century Society (020 7250 3857; www.c20society.org.uk) for further information.

Books and other reference material

There is a wide range of books on fire brigade history, firefighting, insurance brigades and appliances available. A good website at www.firebookshop.co.uk stocks a range of titles, including many firefighting memoirs and histories of individual county brigades, providing more information about fire station buildings and their history.

A guidance note on managing *London's Historic Fire Stations* (Historic England, 2010) is available to download: historicengland.org.uk/images-books/publications/londons-historic-fire-stations. This guidance outlines the history of the fire station and gives further practical information on the management of active historic fire stations as well as caring for decommissioned fire stations in alternative uses.

If you are researching the fire stations of a particular location, the best resource would be British History Online (www.british-history.ac.uk), which includes an overview of the history of public service provision for most parts of the UK.

There is a range of fire brigade history groups on Facebook, UK Fire Brigade History being a prominent one. All of the sixty-three modern brigades also have an online presence.

Kevin Hale's encyclopaedic website (www.firestations.org.uk) has details of every fire station ever operated in the UK and is a fantastic online resource with photographs, links and historical information. You can upload your own images of fire stations old and new.

In addition, the Fire Brigade Society (www.thefirebrigadesociety.co.uk) is a membership organisation that celebrates all aspects of firefighting, and exists to foster interest in fire and rescue services, fire stations and more. They produce an acclaimed journal, *Fire Cover*, as well as area newsletters, and host regular area meetings and a range of events annually.

Other books include:

Henderson, Ronald, *British Steam Fire Engines* (Amberley Books, 2016). *Written by an expert on steam engines, this book tells the story of the development of early British steam fire engines – a fascinating insight to early industrial technology.*

Hutchinson, Barry, *Dennis Fire Engines* (Amberley Books, 2015). *Charts the development and production of one of the most famous fire engine manufacturers in the world, from 1908 to the present day.*

LFB, *One Hundred and Fifty Years of London Fire Brigade in Pictures* (2016). *London Fire Brigade produced a beautifully illustrated, limited edition photo-book in their anniversary year, to celebrate 150 years of service.*

Wright, Brian, *Insurance Fire Brigades 1680–1929* (Tempus Publishing Ltd, 2008). *This comprehensive book focuses on the history of British insurance brigades and gives a wealth of detail about their organisation and operation over 250 years.*

Places to visit

A number of good fire brigade museums operate across the country, often housed in former fire stations, showcasing the architecture of the fire brigade.

London Fire Brigade Museum, rear of 8 Albert Embankment

020 8555 1200; www.london-fire.gov.uk/london-fire-brigade-museum.asp

This free museum currently operates from the old workshops at the rear of the site, with future plans to extend into part of the old fire station. Alongside modern and historic appliances, the museum displays photographic and video archives. Free guided tours are available.

The Museum of Fire, 76–78 Lauriston Place, Edinburgh

www.firescotland.gov.uk/about-us/our-heritage.aspx

In 2018 the Edinburgh Museum of Fire is moving to a new purpose-built facility at McDonald Road fire station, where it resided for twenty-five years prior to moving to Lauriston Place. The new museum will combine modern and interactive displays with historical artefacts relating to over 400 years of firefighting history.

The Scottish Fire and Rescue Service Museum, the Old Fire Station, Dalrymple Street, Greenock.

01698 300 999; www.sfrheritagetrust.org

Telling the story of firefighting in the West of Scotland, the SFRS museum also displays one of the largest collections of fire marks in the UK. They regularly exhibit their historic appliances at events across the region.

The National Emergency Services Museum, Old Police and Fire Station, West Bar, Sheffield
0114 2491 999; www.emergencymuseum.org.uk

The museum includes exhibits and vehicles from all of the Emergency Services, and tells the story of the services and how they work together. They work closely with the Ambulance Heritage Society, based in Nottingham. The NES Museum is also currently working up plans to open a new museum in Cornwall.

The Welsh Museum of Fire, Lonlas Village Workshops, Skewen, Neath, South Wales
01639 635761; www.wafersmuseum.org.uk

Run by the Welsh Area Fire Engine Restoration Society (WAFERS), this is one of the largest museums of its type. It has a wide collection of brigade memorabilia and restored fire engines, and you can also view restoration of engines in progress.

The Greater Manchester Fire Service Museum, Maclure Road, Rochdale
01706 341219; gmfsmuseum.org.uk

Located in the former workshops of the Rochdale fire station, the GMFS Museum holds an extensive fleet of historic appliances together with archival information on the Greater Manchester Area fire brigades.

   All of these museums arrange events, educational visits to schools and open days. They all rely on volunteers and offer plenty of opportunities to get involved, from the restoration of historic appliances to archiving to education, so get in touch for further information.

Detail of a fire bucket used as a planter outside the former fire station of the Hungerford Volunteer Fire Brigade, Berkshire.

Middlesbrough community fire station, Cleveland, showing the efficient modern aesthetic of a fire station interior in 2015.

Image Credits

The author and publisher would like to thank the following people / organisations for permission to use copyright material in this book:

Reading Museum: p. 5: Roman force pump.
Getty Images: p. 41: Fire brigade rally at Blenheim Palace; p. 46: Fire Engine constructed by Messrs Dennis Bros; p. 47: the New Rowntree cocoa works fire-engine 1929; p. 48: Makeshift HQ; p. 50: air raid precautions; p. 51: firemen on jumping sheet.
Courtesy of London Fire Brigade/Mary Evans Picture Library: p. 10: firefighting team putting out a fire; p. 13: members of Coventry Volunteer Fire Brigade; p. 25: Chance the firemen's dog, LFEE; p. 26: London Fire Brigade, nineteenth century, horse-drawn steam pump; p. 49: AFS women resting in bunks; p. 50: new NFS subfire station, Bushey District.
James Thomson, Ecus Ltd: p. 18: Southcotes lane fire station, Kingston-upon-Hull.
Historic England Archive: p. 19: town hall, Marlow, Buckinghamshire; p. 22: Old Wharf storehouses, Newbury, W. Berkshire; p. 34: interior view, fire station, Port Sunlight; p. 43: Portsmouth Naval fire station, c. 1900; p. 47: Boots factory, Beeston, Notts.; p. 52: fire station, Drove Road, Swindon; p. 52: Building 66, fire station, RAF Barnham; p. 55: Ops room, central fire station, Liverpool.
Fiona Taylor: p. 32: Fenton; p. 39: Lincoln; p. 39: Wolverhampton.
Steve Mayes Photography: p. 56: Allendale; p. 58: Middlesbrough; P. 59: Marley Park; p. 64: Middlesbrough interior view.
Beth Scaysbrook: p. 42: Lauriston place fire station.
All other images are the author's own or kindly taken by Liz Reading.

Every attempt has been made to seek permission for copyright material used in this book. However, if we have inadvertently used copyright material without permission / acknowledgement we apologise and we will make the necessary correction at the first opportunity.